EARTH IN

A young sorghum plant—a type of grain that is an important food crop—struggles to grow in the parched ground of the Affollé region of Mauritania, south of the Sahara. Climate change has already caused dry areas to become drier, and it may be causing more severe droughts in Africa and other parts of the world.

PRESERVE OUR
PLANET

THE HOT SEAT

BULLETINS FROM A WARMING WORLD

marfé ferguson delano

FEATURING
Robert Barrett, Sylvia Earle, Mark Lynas,
David de Rothschild, Edward O. Wilson

foreword by John Fahey
President and CEO of National Geographic Society

WASHINGTON, D.C.

For Katie, David, and Sarah Bodner
and
Everly and Jake Sherman
and
their marvelous moms

MFD

Author's Acknowledgments

This book is the brainchild of my editor, Jennifer Emmett, and I thank her for giving me the opportunity to write it. Her encouragement, good sense, and unflappable calm helped me throughout the process. Summer intern Jennifer Eaton researched "green tips" and gave the manuscript a careful review. I am grateful for the improvements she suggested. Thanks to Lori Epstein, Bea Jackson, David M. Seager, and Jim Hiscott for creating such a visually compelling book.

I am especially grateful to Dr. Dan Fagre, a research ecologist with the U.S. Geological Survey, for his expert review of the text. Thanks to fact-checker Michelle Harris for her review. Any mistakes that remain are mine alone. Thanks also to Sherri DeCoursey and Karen Wolverton for their careful reading.

My friend Deborah Heiligman gave me sound advice and a sympathetic ear. She also told me about *The Next One Hundred Years,* a book about climate change that her husband, Jonathan Weiner, wrote some 20 years ago. I found the story about Charles Keeling and the mule deer in Jonathan's foresighted and fascinating book, which is now out of print but well worth tracking down at your library or from used-book sellers.

Thanks to the following people at National Geographic and the National Geographic Channel for their help with this project: John Fahey, Nina Hoffman, Mark Bauman, Susan Borke, Meredith Conte, Truly Herbert, Ben Shaw, Beth Foster, Fred Armstrong, Lauren Jones, Seth Bauer, Solvie Karlstrom, Betty Clayman-DeAtley, Melayne Cohen, Jason Orfanon, Dawn Rodney, Christos DeVaris, Susan White Frazier, Jim Choe, Chalkley Calderwood, Chris Albert, Wendy A. Yascur, Cheryl Zook, Kathie Teter, Mark Thiessen, and Ellen Stanley. Thanks also to National Public Radio for their help with the Climate Connections features. **npr** npr.org

For more than 120 years, National Geographic has been committed to preserving our planet. At this very moment, there are hundreds of National Geographic scientists and explorers around the globe making a difference in the conservation of the world's extraordinary habitats and species. Together with them, explore and discover these threatened places and animals...because the more we all know about the world, the more we can do to help preserve it.

Library of Congress Cataloging-in-Publication Data
Delano, Marfe Ferguson.
Earth in the hot seat : bulletins from a warming world / by Marfé Ferguson Delano.—1st ed.
p. cm.
Includes bibliographical references and index.
ISBN 978-1-4263-0434-7 (hardcover : alk. paper)—ISBN 978-1-4263-0435-4 (library binding : alk. paper)
1. Global warming. 2. Global temperature changes. 3. Greenhouse effect, Atmospheric. I. Title.
QC981.8.G56D446 2009
363.738'74—dc22   2008029317

Printed in China

FOREWORD: Climate change is here. It's not something that might happen in the faraway future, it's happening now. Melting glaciers, rising seas, lakes freezing later, and flowers blooming sooner are just a few of the unmistakable signs that our world is changing rapidly. And although global climate has changed many times in Earth's long history, the current warming trend can't be explained by natural cycles alone. There's one thing that's dramatically different from the past: all the carbon dioxide and other greenhouse gases that human activities are sending into the atmosphere. That means that we humans are responsible for climate change. We can also be the ones who keep it from tumbling out of control. The solution starts with caring about the Earth.

For more than a hundred years, National Geographic has been inspiring people to care about our planet. This book by award-winning children's book author Marfé Ferguson Delano embodies that mission. In these pages, she looks at the changes happening all around us and explains the nature and causes of climate change. She explores the challenges that global warming creates and the steps being taken to combat it. Equally important, she shares ways that each of us can help make a difference.

We're doing so many exciting things at National Geographic to help people understand and care for the Earth. You'll see some examples of our research and projects in the special "Bulletins" section following each chapter in this book, and you can find more information about the bulletin features on page 62.

The state of our planet is in our hands. It's up to us all—grown-ups and kids alike—to ensure that it stays a wonderful world for generations to come.

JOHN FAHEY
PRESIDENT AND CEO
NATIONAL GEOGRAPHIC SOCIETY

John Fahey on board a floating classroom on the Anacostia River in Washington, D.C.

Leader of the pack, Greenland hunter Gedion Kristiansen drags his team of dogs toward the frozen sea, where the ice gets thinner and travel gets riskier every year. The dogs resist because they can sense that the sea ice is melting—they can smell the salt water.

THE BIG THAW
SIGNS OF A WARMING WORLD

If you ever want to see the awesome glaciers that gave Montana's Glacier National Park its name, you might want to plan your trip sooner rather than later. Why the rush? Because if you wait too long, you could miss them. A century ago this rugged region of snowy white peaks and valleys was home to 150 glaciers. Not any more. Drip by drip, all but 25 of the huge slabs of ice have totally melted away.

DAN FAGRE, a scientist for the U.S. Geological Survey, has been studying and measuring the glaciers in Glacier National Park for more than 15 years. He predicts that by the year 2030, Glacier National Park will be glacier-free. "It will be the first time in at least 7,000 years that this landscape has not had glaciers," he says.

Montana isn't the only place where ice is changing. From Peru to Switzerland to India, mountain glaciers around the world are shrinking. So are the vast, dome-shaped glaciers, called ice sheets, that blanket most of Antarctica and Greenland. The thick crust of sea ice covering the Arctic Ocean is thinning and shrinking. The big thaw is a clear sign that Earth's climate is heating up. More evidence comes from thermometer records from around the globe. They show that over the past hundred years, the average surface temperature of our planet has risen a little over 1 degree Fahrenheit (0.74 degrees Celsius). This is called global warming, a term you've probably been hearing a lot these days.

One degree may not sound like much, but it's the difference between an ice cube staying solid (at 32 degrees Fahrenheit) or oozing into a puddle (at 33 degrees). So it's not surprising that glaciers and polar ice are melting as Earth's temperature creeps higher. It's how fast they're disappearing that's fascinating— and alarming—scientists. "Things that normally happen in geologic time are happening during the span of a human lifetime. It's like watching the Statue of Liberty melt," says Fagre.

Glaciers are especially sensitive to climate change. Most are found in places that get a lot of snow in the winter and stay cool in the summer, such as high mountain ranges and polar regions. Glaciers always shrink some in the warmth of summer, but as long as the ice that melts away is replaced by enough snowfall in the winter, they survive. Over our

POLAR BARE: SHRINKING SEA ICE

1979

2005

2007

Going, going ... gone? Satellite images reveal the loss of summer sea ice in the Arctic Ocean over the past three decades. Researchers predict the Arctic could be ice free in summer by 2030, and perhaps as soon as 2013.

Huge white blankets draped across a ski slope on Austria's Pitztal Glacier help it keep its cool during the summer months by reflecting sunlight away. Ski resort owners in Germany and Switzerland are also covering up at least part of their glaciers during the summer to help slow summer melting.

planet's long history, glaciers have formed and vanished many times as Earth's climate has naturally cycled in and out of cooler and warmer periods. Normally, however, glaciers change very slowly, over hundreds or even thousands of years. Today Fagre and other scientists are watching them disappear from one summer to the next. "When I go to some of the glaciers I know well, I come over the ridge, and I don't even have to pull out maps or photos," Fagre says. "I can just look and go, Oh my gosh, that whole area's gone."

The meltdown is really zipping along in polar regions, where scientists say average surface temperatures have risen twice as fast as elsewhere on the planet. In parts of Antarctica, huge ice shelves are thinning and breaking up. An ice shelf is part of an ice sheet that spreads out from the coast and floats atop ocean waters. Over the past 30 years, several ice shelves in West

Snow and ice aren't the only things melting in a warming world. This bumpy bike path near Fairbanks, Alaska, was once on level ground, but the thawing of the permafrost—a layer of soil that normally stays permanently frozen—has given rise to all sorts of buckles and bumps as the ground softens.

Antarctica have collapsed into the sea, including a shelf about the size of Rhode Island in 2002. That may be a small state, but it's a humongous hunk of ice. And 30 years may seem like a long time, but in Earth's history that's not even the blink of an eye.

Satellite measurements at the north end of the globe show that the speed of ice loss in Greenland has doubled over the past decade. Konrad Steffen, a climate researcher from the University of Colorado, has witnessed the changes on the frigid island from a front-row seat. Every year since 1993, he has set up camp on Greenland's ice sheet and studied what happens when the heat of spring sunlight starts to melt the surface. Since then, winter temperatures at camp have risen about 9 degrees Fahrenheit (5 degrees Celsius). Once Steffen could ride his snowmobile across firm snow to other research stations as late as May; now he risks getting stuck in slush at that time of year. "The melt season is getting longer, starting earlier, and ending later," Steffen says. A longer, hotter melt season leads to more meltwater surging across the ice sheet. This in turn speeds up the pace of outlet glaciers, which carry ice from the ice sheet's interior out toward the sea. At the edge of the island, huge sections of the glaciers break off and float away as icebergs.

Slide, glide, whoops! Once all ice-skating took place outdoors. Now natural ice thick enough to skate on safely, as this girl and her dad are doing, is hard to come by.

Nowhere has global warming hit harder than in the Arctic Ocean. Most of its waters are covered year-round by a thick layer of sea ice. Like glaciers, this sea ice always retreats some in summer. But in late summer 2007, the permanent ice cover shrank to the smallest it's been since satellite ice surveys began in the late 1970s. The previous low was set in 2005. Between those two years, summertime ice declined by an area larger than the states of Texas and California combined. Sea routes that are normally icebound opened up to ships. Scientists now forecast that as global warming continues, the Arctic Ocean could be ice-free in summer by 2030, and perhaps as early as 2013.

Scientists believe that the shrinking ice and snow cover in the Arctic and other cold regions may actually be speeding up global warming, because of something called the albedo effect. Snow and ice, which are light colored, have a high albedo. That means they reflect a great deal of the sun's rays back into space. Land and open water, which are darker, have a low albedo— they absorb a lot of sunshine. When glaciers and sea ice melt, more land or open water is exposed, so Earth absorbs more heat, like a parking lot on a summer day. This causes even more melting, which leads to more heat being absorbed, which causes more melting, and so on. You could call it a vicious

Leveled by logging, this stretch of Borneo's
rain forest was once green and lush (inset).
The clearing of forests, called deforestation,
is contributing to the warming of our planet.

circle. Climate scientists, or climatologists, call it a feedback loop.

The rapid melting in the Arctic is already affecting the people and wildlife who make their home there. For most of us, however, the changes happening in polar regions may seem far removed from everyday life. Still, depending on where you live, other signs of global warming can be found closer to home. Your parents or grandparents, for example, might recall ice-skating on a local pond or lake when they were kids. If you're hoping to do the same, you may want to think twice before lacing up your skates. Chances are you could end up skating on thin ice, if you can find any at all these days.

Barbara Benson, a scientist from the University of Wisconsin, studies how climate change affects the timing of ice formation and breakup in lakes and rivers. She and her colleagues have pored over a wide variety of sources— including old newspapers and transportation records— documenting ice records for lakes and rivers throughout the Northern Hemisphere for the years 1855 through 2005. Their findings show that over that time, the average number of days the water bodies are covered by ice has decreased dramatically. Today lakes freeze about 12 days later in the fall and thaw about 13 days earlier in the spring than they did 150 years ago. Some lakes that once froze solid during winter now have years in which they don't freeze over at all. Much of the change, Benson and the other scientists believe, is due to global warming.

Following the leader, geese wing their way north. Geese are among the many birds that now migrate earlier in the spring, if they migrate at all.

Earth's rising temperature has also influenced the schedules of plants and animals in many places around the world. Compared to just 50 years ago, birds are migrating north earlier in spring, insects are hatching earlier, flowers are blooming sooner, and crops are ripening sooner by days, weeks, or even months. All these behaviors are more signs of global warming, say scientists. And most of them agree that human activity—in particular the burning of so-called fossil fuels and the clearing of forests—has contributed in a big way to the rapid warming that is changing our planet before our eyes.

CLIMATE CONNECTIONS

npr
npr.org
NATIONAL GEOGRAPHIC

AN ADÉLIE PENGUIN LEAPS FROM AN ICEBERG.

Penguins Helped and Hurt by Changing Climate

DURING THE PAST FEW DECADES, as climate patterns in parts of Antarctica have changed dramatically, Adélie penguins in some regions have almost disappeared. But the Adélies in Cape Royds, Antarctica, are doing better than ever. "These penguins are definitely being helped by climate change," says scientist David Ainley. He and other researchers think they know why. Most types of penguins go fishing only in open water, so they're all competing with each other to find food. But Adélies catch their fish by diving deep under the ice. In fact, they're just about the only penguins that do that. So, when there's plenty of ice over the sea, Adélies hardly have any competition and they can get all the food they want. Now the changing climate is shaking things up. In some areas where most of the ice has melted, Adélies can't survive. But Cape Royds used to have too much ice, and now it has just the right amount. So penguins here are doing great. Ainley says here's the moral: Global warming is making life unpredictable.

— Adapted from Climate Connections report, ©2008, NPR®. All Rights Reserved.

HUMAN FOOTPRINT

Everything you eat. Everything you drink. Everything you use. Your entire life's consumption. In one place at one time.

A river of yellow, these **28,433** rubber ducks represent the number of showers taken by the average American in a lifetime. If each of those **28,433** showers lasts **5** minutes, the amount of water used is equal to running the water nonstop for **98** days. If they last **7** minutes each, that's equal to running the water nonstop for **136** days.

GREEN GUIDE
HOT TIPS TO FIGHT GLOBAL WARMING

Share these energy-saving tips with your parents!

- Place your desk next to a window and use natural light instead of a lamp.

- Switch off the light every time you leave a room.

- When it gets hot in the summer, use a fan instead of turning on the air conditioner. If you must use the AC, set the thermostat no lower than 78 degrees, and keep the fan buzzing to stay cool.

- Wear more layers in winter instead of cranking up the heat.

EARTH'S VOICES

Edward O. Wilson Speaks Out

Harvard professor Edward O. Wilson is a biologist, writer, and conservationist, as well as one of the world's leading authorities on ants. He has been a champion for biodiversity and once wrote, "When you have seen one ant, one bird, one tree, you have not seen them all." He won the 1978 Pulitzer Prize for his book, On Human Nature, *and the 1990 Pulitzer Prize for* The Ants, *with Bert Hölldobler.*

What is your favorite place on Earth?
The wonderful forests and shores of northwest Florida and South Alabama, where I grew up.

What advice do you have for kids about reversing global warming?
First, learn about it. Talk with others about it. As you get older, use your voice and make your own effort to help move us all toward the greening of America, using clean new energy sources and ways of life that use less energy.

What is your favorite animal?
Why, ants of course, because I've spent almost my whole life studying ants. My favorite ants are the big, ferocious bulldog ants of Australia. They have big eyes and chase you if you get too close to their nest.

The world would be a better place if ...
We all really, truly loved the rest of life on Earth. If we take care to preserve all the endangered species of plants and animals and the habitats they live in, the world would be a better place for them—and for us!

Just 15% of Americans say they always minimize the use of freshwater, compared with four in ten Brazilians (41%), a third of Australians (35%), and three in ten Germans (29%), French (28%), and Mexicans (27%).

SIX°DEGREES
COULD CHANGE THE WORLD

1 IF GLOBAL WARMING GOES UNCHECKED AND THE EARTH WARMS **DEGREE CELSIUS** (1.8 Degrees Fahrenheit):

■ The western United States will suffer severe droughts—long dry spells—and people living there will face water shortages.

■ Hurricanes are expected to hit the coastlines of the Mediterranean Sea and the South Atlantic Ocean, which typically do not experience them.

■ People living on tiny Pacific island nations such as Tuvalu will begin to move away for good as rising sea levels submerge their homelands bit by bit.

6
5
4
3
2
1

FOR MORE INFORMATION ABOUT THESE ☐ NATIONAL GEOGRAPHIC INITIATIVES, PLEASE SEE PAGE 62.

On an Austrian mountaintop, scientist Daniela Hohenwallner searches for small clues to the big picture of global warming by taking samples of mosses. Rapid warming in high mountains is causing some plants to shift to higher, cooler ground.

THE BIG PICTURE

THE SCIENCE OF CLIMATE CHANGE

O n May 18, 1955, a 27-year-old chemist named Charles David Keeling and his wife, Louise, went camping along the Big Sur River in California for a couple of days. They took their camping gear, their two-month-old son, Drew, and a box of hollow, sphere-shaped glass flasks. About every four hours, Keeling opened the stopper on one of the flasks and let the container fill with cool Big Sur air. He filled nine flasks.

It's been said that the science of climate change was born on that trip. At the time, most researchers assumed that carbon dioxide gas, or CO_2, released by the burning of fossil fuels such as coal and oil would be absorbed by Earth's oceans, not the atmosphere. Keeling decided to check whether this was correct. Over the next few months, he and his family camped in several other wilderness areas. At each site, the young scientist filled more flasks with air.

Back in his lab at the California Institute of Technology in Pasadena, Keeling measured each sample to see how much carbon dioxide it contained. He recorded his findings in a green notebook. During a campout at Yosemite National Park, that notebook almost became a meal for a hungry mule deer. When a rustling sound awoke him one night, Keeling turned on his flashlight and saw "two big eyes, looking right at me! It was that darn mule deer...and he had my research notebook between his teeth." After chasing the animal, Keeling finally found his notebook on the ground. The deer had left big teeth marks in the pages, but at least it hadn't devoured the data.

To Keeling's surprise, this data showed that the amount of carbon dioxide in the air was nearly the same no matter where a sample had been taken. He realized that meant he could measure the gas in just one place and it would reflect the big picture, the average carbon dioxide level for the whole planet. If he took such measurements year after year, he could see how that level changed over time.

That's what he did. First he devised instruments that could take very precise, continuous carbon dioxide measurements. Then he had them installed at a weather station atop a Hawaiian volcano called Mauna Loa, far away from pollution-spewing cities and factories. Year after year, from 1958 until his death in 2005, Keeling supervised the measurements. They're still going on today. And what the Mauna Loa record, now known in graph form as the "Keeling curve," shows beyond a doubt is that the amount of carbon dioxide in Earth's atmosphere is going up.

It's clear that Earth's temperature is going up, too. Using thermometer

Computer models, like the ones above showing ocean-current temperatures, help scientists to understand how Earth's climate is changing and to predict what's ahead for our planet.

records from thousands of locations on land and at sea, scientists have determined that the global average surface temperature has risen by a little over 1 degree Fahrenheit (0.74 degree Celsius) in the past century. About three-fourths of that increase has occurred in the past 30 years. The rise in both carbon dioxide and temperature is no coincidence, say scientists. Indeed, most of the warming is linked to the buildup of carbon dioxide in the atmosphere. The reason has to do with the greenhouse effect.

Greenhouses are buildings with a glass roof and sides that let sunlight pass through and then trap its warmth inside. This makes a greenhouse a

You can't miss the soot, steam, and other gases spewing from a coal-burning power plant in Conesville, Ohio. What's invisible is the heat-trapping carbon dioxide gas also being released.

great place to grow flowers and other plants during wintertime, when it's too cold for them to survive outdoors. Earth's atmosphere works in kind of the same way. It is made up of water vapor, carbon dioxide, methane, and other gases, including the oxygen we breathe. When sunlight reaches the atmosphere, some of it is reflected back into space and some of it passes through to Earth's surface, which absorbs the incoming light and turns it into heat. The warmed surface then releases, or radiates, heat back into the air. Carbon dioxide and other so-called greenhouse gases absorb some of this rising heat, trapping it in the atmosphere. This keeps our planet warm and cozy, just right for plants and animals to exist. Without the greenhouse effect, Earth's average temperature would be far below freezing—around 0 degrees Fahrenheit (minus 18 degrees Celsius)—instead of the comfortable 59 degrees Fahrenheit (15 degrees Celsius) it is today.

The greenhouse effect is Earth's natural climate-control system. The problem, according to Harvard professor and climate researcher Steven Wofsy, is that "we humans are monkeying with it." How so? We're fiddling with the balance of the system by adding extra carbon dioxide and other greenhouse gases to the atmosphere. The human-caused buildup began around 200 years ago during the time known as the Industrial Revolution, when the invention of new manufacturing and transportation technologies led to the widespread use of fossil fuels. Cotton mills and trains, for example, were powered by coal-burning steam engines. The development of the incandescent lightbulb in 1879 led to coal-burning electric power plants. A few decades later, gasoline-powered automobiles began rolling off assembly lines and onto roads everywhere.

Fossil fuels were formed by the remains of animals and plants that died hundreds of millions of years ago. Like all living things, including you and me, these animals and plants contained carbon, an element often called the building block of life. After they died, they gradually became buried deeper and deeper below the ground or ocean floor. The weight of the dirt or seawater above pressed down on their remains, which gave off heat as they decomposed. Eventually the heat and pressure transformed the dead matter into coal (a solid), oil (a liquid), or natural gas (take a wild guess). When fossil fuels are taken out of the Earth and burned—in power plants or car engines, for example—the carbon that is bound up in them is released into the air. Much of this freed carbon then combines with oxygen to form carbon dioxide. And the more CO_2 and other heat-trapping gases there are in the atmosphere, the warmer our climate system gets.

The widespread clearing of Earth's forests, known as deforestation, also contributes to greenhouse gas emissions. Trees and other plants naturally absorb carbon dioxide from the atmosphere. They convert it back into

THE GREENHOUSE EFFECT

Heat from the sun travels to Earth

When the earth's surface cools, it gives off heat

Some heat is reflected by the atmosphere before reaching Earth's surface

Most heat is absorbed by the earth's surface, warming it

Some heat escapes through the atmosphere

Some is absorbed by the atmosphere, warming it

Some heat is reflected by the atmosphere

Some is absorbed by greenhouse gases

Increased greenhouse gases in the atmosphere trap more and more heat, causing temperatures on Earth to rise

Ice core samples drilled out of Peru's Quelccaya Ice Cap and other glaciers around the world give scientists a window into past climate conditions. If Quelccaya continues to melt at the current rate, ice core samples could be all that remain of it by the year 2100.

carbon, which they store in their leaves and roots, and oxygen, which is released back into the air. Because forests soak up so much carbon, they are known as "carbon sinks." Unfortunately, more than 80 percent of Earth's natural forests have been destroyed by logging, fires, and land clearing for agriculture and animal grazing. Because there are fewer trees to capture CO_2, greater amounts of the gas are entering the atmosphere.

Between deforestation and the use of fossil fuels, humans cause the release of eight billion tons of carbon a year, an amount that continues to increase. This means that greenhouse gas concentration in the atmosphere will continue to rise, and temperatures probably will too. In 1958, the first year of Charles David Keeling's Mauna Loa study, the CO_2 level measured about 315 parts per million (ppm). In 2007 it reached 384 ppm. Scientists believe a little over half of human-produced CO_2 goes into the atmosphere, which accounts for the rise in Keeling's curve. Most of the rest of it goes into another carbon sink, the ocean. It really does absorb a lot of CO_2, just not as much of it as researchers once assumed. All that extra CO_2 is making ocean water more acidic, which scientists say could harm some shelled creatures.

The amount of carbon dioxide in Earth's atmosphere is higher now than it's been in the past 800,000 years, say scientists. You may wonder how they can see so far back into the past. One way involves drilling out

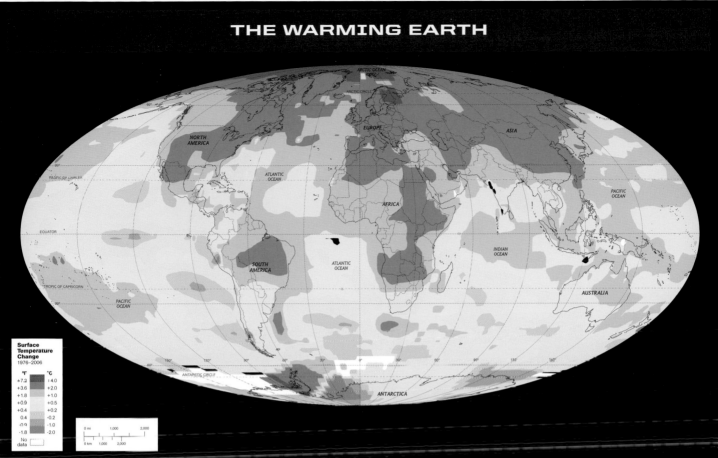

THE WARMING EARTH

Surface Temperature Change 1976–2006

°F	°C
+7.2	+4.0
+3.6	+2.0
+1.8	+1.0
+0.9	+0.5
+0.4	+0.2
-0.4	-0.2
-0.9	-1.0
-1.8	-2.0
No data	

This map shows the change in surface temperatures on Earth from the year 1976 to 2006. As the colors indicate, much of our planet is warmer now than it was 30 years ago. The Arctic is heating up faster than anywhere else on the globe, as its reflective cover of ice and snow shrinks. The Indian Ocean and western Pacific Ocean are warmer than they've been in 11,500 years. In some parts of the oceans, however, deepwater welling up from below has cooled temperatures.

long cylinders, or cores, of ice from the Antarctic ice sheet. Ancient air bubbles trapped in the layers of ice reveal the year-by-year concentration of greenhouse gases in Earth's past atmosphere, as well as the planet's average yearly temperature. These records show that CO_2 levels have risen and fallen in step with global temperatures, as Earth's climate has cycled through ice ages and warmer periods. What makes the current climate change so unpredictable is that never before in those 800,000 years has CO_2 climbed so fast and so far ahead of temperature.

Ice cores aren't the only windows into past climate conditions. The widths of the rings in tree trunks give scientists information about what annual temperatures were like hundreds or even thousands of years ago. Researchers also find keys to climate history in pollen buried under lake beds, stalagmites in caves, and corals in the ocean.

We humans are responsible for sending other greenhouse gases besides CO_2 into the air. The trash we bury in landfills, for example, produces

Just south of the Sahara, a group of women in Mali sing and pray for rain to end the long drought that is drying up their lakes and shriveling their crops. Climate change, deforestation, and drought are turning their homeland into desert, a process known as desertification. In the next decade, food and water shortages caused by desertification could force 50 million people, many of them in Africa, to seek new places to live.

EXTREME WEATHER

If Hurricane Wilma is a sign of things to come in a warming world, Earth could be in for a wild ride. Shown swirling off the coast of Central America on October 19, 2005, the category 5 storm was the most intense hurricane ever recorded in the Atlantic Ocean.

methane. The cows and sheep we raise also burp out this gas. The chemical fertilizers many of us use on our crops and lawns release a greenhouse gas called nitrous oxide. Greenhouse gases have natural sources, of course. Volcanoes spew CO_2 in the air, and animals—including people—exhale it when they breathe. Methane is released naturally by the oceans. Permafrost, the layer of frozen soil and rock in Arctic regions, releases methane and CO_2 when it thaws.

Using computer models that take into account the effects of various factors—including ocean currents, volcanic activity, and greenhouse

During one of the highest tides of 2007, swelling seas swamp the streets and send children fleeing to higher ground on the tiny, low-lying island nation of Tuvalu in the South Pacific Ocean. The dangers of rising sea levels and more severe storms brought on by climate change could eventually leave the 12,000 or so people of Tuvalu no choice but to abandon their home and move to other countries.

gases—on climate, researchers predict that Earth's average temperature could climb by 3.2 to 11.5 degrees Fahrenheit (1.8 to 6.4 degrees Celsius) by the year 2100. What's less certain is how fast this will happen and what it will mean for the planet. Different places will be affected by climate change in different ways. Some places may become wetter, others drier, some warmer, and some may even become cooler.

We can count on one thing for sure. As Earth heats up, sea levels around the world will continue to rise. This is partly because seawater expands as it warms, and partly because runoff from melting mountain glaciers and polar ice sheets adds more water to the oceans. As a result, coastal areas will almost certainly flood more often. Scientists believe that climate change resulting from global warming will also cause more extreme weather, such as hurricanes and cyclones, which intensify over warm waters. And we're already seeing more heat waves, wildfires, and droughts (long periods without rain).

Much remains unknown about global warming, but it's already affecting life on every continent and in every ocean.

CLIMATE CONNECTIONS

npr.org
NATIONAL GEOGRAPHIC

A BUSY SHIPPING AREA—THE PANAMA CANAL

Shallow Water Ahead for the Panama Canal

THE PANAMA CANAL is the shortcut between the Atlantic and the Pacific oceans. It is currently being expanded to accommodate the bigger vessels being used by shipping firms. But the canal may soon face another problem, and here's the climate connection. To fill its locks, the canal depends on fresh water, which pours into the canal from 17 artificial, interconnected lakes. Reduced rainfall brought on by climate change might mean those lakes—and thus the canal—could run out of water. That's not the only way climate change looms over the future of the canal. Melting ice in the Arctic could eventually open up a reliable shipping passage through northern seas. If the world gets warm enough, goods headed for some U.S. ports may skip Panama altogether.

— Adapted from Climate Connections report, ©2008, NPR®. All Rights Reserved.

HUMAN FOOTPRINT

Everything you eat. Everything you drink. Everything you use. Your entire life's consumption. In one place at one time.

What takes **4.5** trees, **715** pounds of plastic, and **1,898** pints of oil to make? The average number of disposable diapers used by an American baby. The grand total comes to **3,796** diapers.

GREEN GUIDE

HOT TIPS TO FIGHT GLOBAL WARMING

Share these energy-saving tips with your parents!

- Shave your eight-minute shower to five minutes for a savings of 513 pounds of CO_2 per year.

- Clean the clutter off your refrigerator. Stuff piled on top of it can prevent your fridge from venting heat effectively, and that wastes energy.

- Choose organically grown produce whenever possible. In one year, the carbon in one acre of organic crop soil will pull up to 7,000 pounds of CO_2 from the atmosphere.

EARTH'S VOICES

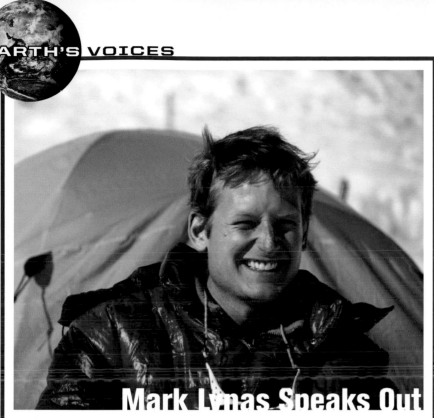

Mark Lynas Speaks Out

Mark Lynas, a National Geographic Emerging Explorer, is a journalist, environmental activist, and the author of the book, Six Degrees: Our Future on a Hotter Planet.

What is your favorite place on Earth?
I have several. A very special one is the Peruvian Cordillera Blanca—the high glaciated mountains east of the town of Huaraz. A second is the Norwegian fjords, with their wonderful cliffs and ice caps. A third is where I live near Oxford, England, in a small village called Wolvercote, which has lots of hidden special places.

What advice do you have for kids about global warming?
The best thing kids can do is lean on adults. Use some pester power to get grown-ups to take the problem more seriously. They can vote, after all.

Have you seen global warming at work?
I've seen global warming in many places. In the islands of Tuvalu I stood in floodwaters as the sea levels rose. In Peru I went to visit a glacier my father had photographed 20 years earlier and found that it had disappeared. Here in Oxford we're seeing much heavier rains and frequent floods—half of our village is constantly threatened by the river rising.

What do you do to help stop global warming?
The biggest thing I do to try and stop global warming is to tell people about it—in books, lectures, and on the radio or television. But I also try to get my own life in order: We don't have a car, and I go almost everywhere by bike or train. We even travel abroad by train, and don't ever fly for holidays. We use green power for electricity and buy local food. I don't see any of these things as a sacrifice. In fact we have a great quality of life. I'd much rather go to the farmers market and talk to people I know than go to a supermarket where I don't know anyone.

What is the one thing you wish kids knew about global warming?
That it is much easier to fix than most adults make out.

Six in ten Americans (59%) drive alone daily. Six in ten Australians (61%) and six in ten French (62%) do the same. Among those surveyed, the Chinese are by far the least likely to drive by themselves most days (8%).

Greendex™

SIX°DEGREES
COULD CHANGE THE WORLD

2 IF GLOBAL WARMING GOES UNCHECKED AND THE EARTH WARMS **DEGREES CELSIUS** (3.6 Degrees Fahrenheit):

- Polar bears will struggle to survive as glaciers increasingly melt away.

- Coral reefs will vanish as sea temperatures rise.

- Greenland's vast ice sheet could tip into a rapid, irreversible meltdown, leading to a rise in global sea levels.

- In India, production of rice and wheat may fall dramatically.

- On the positive side, in Europe warmth-loving crops like sunflowers and soybeans will be able to grow much farther north.

FOR MORE INFORMATION ABOUT THESE ☐ NATIONAL GEOGRAPHIC INITIATIVES, PLEASE SEE PAGE 62.

There's nowhere to run—or hop—for the strawberry tree frog of Ecuador to escape the effects of climate change. Like many other cloud forest frogs, it is becoming increasingly rare.

FEELING THE HEAT

LIFE IN A WARMER WORLD

The Monteverde Cloud Forest Preserve in Costa Rica teems with amazing wildlife. Jaguars, ocelots, and a wide variety of hummingbirds and butterflies are among the many creatures that thrive in the cool, misty mountaintop forest. For a million years or so, it was also home to the Monteverde harlequin frog, a species found nowhere else on Earth. Not anymore. The last time anyone spotted one of these tiny, brightly colored amphibians was in the late 1980s. Its cousin, the golden toad, vanished around the same time. It too was found only in the Monteverde Cloud Forest. Ecologist J. Alan Pounds, a resident scientist at the preserve, has studied wildlife there for more than 25 years. He and his colleagues believe the disappearance of both creatures is linked to climate change caused by global warming.

The warming trend of the past 30 years, say scientists, has increased evaporation in the tropical mountains, and this has caused more clouds to form over them. In the daytime, the extra cloud cover blocks sunlight, so temperatures stay cooler than they once were. At night, the cloud cover serves as a blanket, holding in heat. These cooler days and warmer nights are ideal conditions for the spread of a naturally occurring fungus called chytrid, which invades the thin skin of amphibians and kills them. Alan Pounds believes the deadly disease is responsible for wiping out dozens of harlequin frog species and other amphibians across Central and South America. He explains it this way: "Disease is the bullet killing frogs, but climate change is pulling the trigger."

Habitat loss, pollution, overhunting, and overfishing already threaten much of Earth's wildlife. Now scientists are finding signs that our planet's animals and plants are also feeling the heat from human-caused climate change. "We're seeing impacts on every continent and every ocean," says Camille Parmesan, a biologist at the University of Texas. Parmesan tracks the effects of climate change on wildlife all over the globe. According to her calculations, more than half of the world's wild species have been affected in one way or another by the rapid warming that's occurred over the last century.

Many plants and animals are finding ways to adapt to climate change. Parmesan and her colleagues estimate that about 60 percent of all plants and animals show changes in the timing of such events as breeding, flowering, or migration. In response to warmer average temperatures, for example, the famous cherry trees in Washington, D.C., now blossom about a week earlier than they did 30 years ago. In Great Britain, birds are laying their eggs an average of nine days earlier than in the mid-20th century.

Many animals are trying to beat the heat by moving to a cooler

Edith's checkerspot butterfly

home. Take the Edith's checkerspot butterfly, a small insect found throughout the American West. Over the past century, the checkerspot has abandoned its southernmost habitats in Mexico and southern California and has shifted its range farther north in Canada. This happened right in step with rising temperatures.

Red fox

Plants are on the move, too. Of course, they can't just pick up and fly or crawl or slither away, but the seeds and spores they spread can grow better in one place than another. Researchers in mountainous regions report that a warming climate is causing many cold-loving mosses, herbs, and ferns to inch up hillsides to higher elevations, where it's cooler. The problem is, those mountaintop areas are already inhabited by other plants. In the competition for survival in a limited space, some species are bound to be losers.

Speaking of competition, scientists expect to see a lot more of it, as more and more species crowd into cooler zones. In Canada, Norway, and Sweden, for example, red foxes are shifting their range hundreds of miles closer to the North Pole, into the territories of Arctic foxes. The red foxes are taking over their Arctic cousins' dens and competing with them for food. The red invaders have even been observed killing Arctic foxes.

As different plants and animals react to global warming in different ways, the natural rhythms of species that depend on each other are falling out of beat. For instance, some plants have started blooming before the insects that pollinate them become active. In the Rocky Mountains, the large rodents known as yellow-bellied marmots used to hibernate until mid-May. Now they often emerge from their burrows in mid-April, when the plants they feed on may still be buried under snow. "When they get up early in years with a dense snowpack, they starve or are eaten by predators," says biologist Dan Blumstein of the Rocky Mountain Biological Laboratory in Colorado.

For some creatures—such as the harlequin frog and the golden toad—climate change is happening faster than they can adapt to it. As a result, many of these species are dying out, or going extinct. "What surprises me most is that it has happened so soon," says Parmesan. In addition to cloud-forest frogs, she notes, some types of butterflies, ocean corals, and polar birds have already gone extinct, largely due to global warming.

The species hit hardest by climate change are those that live in narrow geographic areas—such as cloud forests—and those that make their home in cold climates, such as polar regions or mountaintops. Polar bears, walruses, and ringed seals in the Arctic all depend on sea ice as a platform for feeding and raising their young. So do penguins in the Antarctic. If temperatures

Damaged by warming seas, this coral reef in the Indian Ocean offers poor shelter for passing fish. It looks like a graveyard compared to healthy coral (inset).

continue to rise and sea ice continues to shrink, as climatologists predict, these cold-loving creatures may one day be unable to survive in the wild. There's no place for them to go. The U.S. Geological Service predicts that more than two-thirds of the world's polar bear population could vanish within 50 years if their icy habitat continues to melt away.

On the other hand, some species are loving life in a warmer world. Mountain pine beetles are reproducing more often and moving into mountains and forests that were once too cold for them. Since winter temperatures on average are higher these days, more of the bugs are surviving over the winter. That's tough luck for pine trees. The exploding pine beetle population is chewing up millions of acres of pines across the western U.S. and Canada. Meanwhile, poison ivy is growing like crazy in a warmer world. Researchers say the increased carbon dioxide in the air seems to help the weed to grow faster and bigger and to produce more of the oil that makes so many of us itch like crazy.

Ocean life is also being greatly affected by global warming. About half the carbon dioxide released into the air by the burning of fossil fuels is being absorbed by ocean water. When carbon dioxide mixes with water, it forms carbonic acid. That's the same stuff that makes soda pop fizzy. It's also the same stuff that helps soda dissolve your teeth if you drink too much of it! The more CO_2 the oceans absorb, the more acidic they become. That spells trouble for coral reefs and other shell-building sea life. The increased acidity interferes with the calcium compound these creatures need to build and maintain their shells and skeletons. If ocean acidity continues to rise at the current rate, say scientists, by the end of this century it may be powerful enough to dissolve the shells of some small creatures, such as the pteropod snail.

Oceans aren't just getting more acidic; they're also getting warmer as global temperatures rise. Many marine species are responding by moving closer to the poles, where the water is cooler. Corals, however, are stuck in place. These tropical sea dwellers are very sensitive to changes in temperature. When the water gets too hot for comfort, they shed the algae that nourish them. This process is called bleaching, because

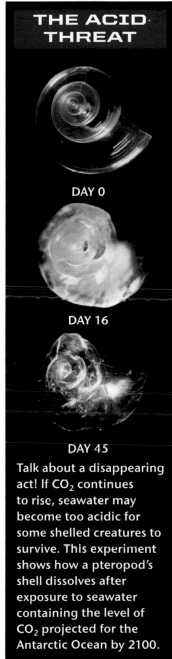

THE ACID THREAT

DAY 0

DAY 16

DAY 45
Talk about a disappearing act! If CO_2 continues to rise, seawater may become too acidic for some shelled creatures to survive. This experiment shows how a pteropod's shell dissolves after exposure to seawater containing the level of CO_2 projected for the Antarctic Ocean by 2100.

it leaves the coral white. Reefs can recover from bleaching if cooler water temperatures return soon enough. Unfortunately, as average ocean temperatures rise, bleaching episodes are becoming more frequent—and more deadly. Because so many fish and other sea creatures depend on coral reefs for food, shelter, and as a place to raise their young, reef destruction could throw the ocean food chain off balance.

People who make their home in Arctic regions are among the humans most affected by global warming so far. Thinning, shifting sea ice makes it more dangerous—if not downright impossible—for hunters in Greenland and other Arctic lands to travel over the ice in search of their traditional game of seals, walrus, and polar bears. As a result, many native people of the Arctic are turning to other ways to make a living and feed their families. In Scandinavia and Russia, later freezes and earlier thaws are making it harder for Sami reindeer herders to manage the animals on which their age-old way of life depends.

As glaciers melt and warming seawater expands, more people in places around the world face flooding. The average global sea level has already increased by four to eight inches in the last century, according to the Intergovernmental Panel on Climate

Meltwater gushes off the Greenland ice sheet. If the ice sheet were to totally collapse—which scientists believe is unlikely in this century—the water from the ice sheet alone would raise sea level by 23 feet.

Change (IPCC), a group of hundreds of the world's leading climate-change scientists. The IPCC estimates that if global warming continues, seas could rise another 7 to 24 inches—and perhaps higher—by 2100. People who live in low-lying coastal areas will be hit hardest by rising waters. Some small islands in the South Pacific could be swallowed up whole by the ocean.

If humans do nothing to fight global warming, say scientists, we're likely to face many other challenges as a result of climate change. The millions of people in India, Peru, and Bolivia who now depend on runoff from glaciers for drinking water, crop irrigation, and hydroelectric power will face water shortages as glaciers shrivel up. Climate change is already causing dry areas such as the American Southwest and southern Africa to become even drier. In a worst-case scenario, according to the IPCC, climate change could cause widespread crop failure and lead to worldwide food shortages.

The good news is that humankind can do something about climate change. We can't make it go away, but we do have the ability to limit the impact of global warming. There's no time to waste, however, if we want to keep our planet a lovely place for life.

A wildfire blazes through a forest in Idaho. As Earth heats up, wildfires are on the rise and wildlife is on the run.

CLIMATE CONNECTIONS

npr.org
NATIONAL GEOGRAPHIC

TUAREG TRIBESMEN CROSS THE SAHARA WITH THEIR CAMELS.

Drought Forces Desert Nomads to Settle Down

FOR CENTURIES, Africa's Tuareg people have lived as nomads, herding their animals from field to field just south of the Sahara Desert in Mali, near Timbuktu. "Our life is basically the animals we have, so we protect them and we feed them," says Mohamed Ag Mustafa, a Tuareg herder. "Whenever we need tea or grain or clothes, we take an animal to the market and sell it and buy something." Over the past 40 years, however, a change in climate has forced the Tuareg to give up their wandering way of life. A severe drought has made it more difficult to find grazing for their animals. To survive, the Tuareg have had to start settling in villages and farming. They are trying to maintain their traditions while learning a new way of life, but this may be the end of a culture.

—*Adapted from Climate Connections report, ©2007, NPR®. All Rights Reserved.*

HUMAN FOOTPRINT

Everything you eat. Everything you drink. Everything you use. Your entire life's consumption. In one place at one time.

Got milk? These cartons represent the amount of milk the average American drinks during a lifetime: **26,112** glasses. There are **9.2** million American cows producing milk. Getting their milk from the dairy to your fridge takes a lot of energy, so don't waste a drop of it!

GREEN GUIDE

HOT TIPS TO FIGHT GLOBAL WARMING

Share these energy-saving tips with your parents!

- Trim down on the amount of the red meat you eat. Since it takes more fossil fuels to produce red meat than fish, eggs and poultry, switching to these foods will slim your CO_2 emissions.

- Take the bus, ride your bike, or walk instead of using the car. On average, you produce roughly one pound of CO_2 for every mile driven in an automobile.

- Always recycle. Recycling paper, plastic, and glass can reduce CO_2 emissions by 1,000 pounds each year.

EARTH'S VOICES

Sylvia Earle Speaks Out

Sylvia Earle is an oceanographer, explorer, and author. She has led more than 60 expeditions and logged more than 6,000 hours underwater.

What is your favorite place on Earth?
I love all wild places, from the deep sea to deserts. The wilder, the wetter, the better.

What advice do you have for kids about global warming?
First, learn about it and understand how everything is connected. Whatever can be done to reduce CO_2 emissions helps. Walking or using a bicycle instead of driving seems a small thing, but multiplied by millions of individual actions, it adds up to a big number.

Have you seen global warming at work?
I have seen many coral reefs that are affected by bleaching, something that appears to be connected to warming of the ocean.

What is your favorite animal?
I love them all, but have a special fondness for groupers of all sorts. These fish are exceedingly curious and sometimes follow me around underwater like puppies. I am also particularly fond of four wondrous primate animals, my grandsons.

What do you do to help stop global warming?
First, I try to make people aware of the issues by speaking, writing, and sharing photographs of species and places that need help. I am doing whatever I can to bring about protection of the natural world on the land and in the ocean. I drive a hybrid car, eat low on the food chain, and generally do whatever I can to reduce my personal carbon "flipper-print."

How big is your carbon footprint?
It is larger than I would like, owing to an enormous amount of air travel. For many meetings and for ocean exploration, there is really no substitute for being there.

The world would be a better place if ...
We treated the natural world—wild creatures and wild places—as if our lives depended on them, because they do.

Four in ten U.S. consumers say they always recycle (38%), far fewer than consumers in Canada (59%), Australia (59%), Great Britain (54%), and Germany (53%), where rates top more than half of the population.

SIX DEGREES
COULD CHANGE THE WORLD

3 IF GLOBAL WARMING GOES UNCHECKED AND THE EARTH WARMS **DEGREES CELSIUS** (5.4 Degrees Fahrenheit):

- The North Pole could be ice-free during the summer.

- The Amazon rain forest is likely to dry out and eventually become more like a desert.

- The southern half of Africa will get less and less rain, causing widespread crop failures and starvation.

- Farmers may try to cultivate ice-free Arctic soil, but are likely to be unsuccessful.

- Drought and food shortages could force millions to leave Central America.

FOR MORE INFORMATION ABOUT THESE ◻ NATIONAL GEOGRAPHIC INITIATIVES, PLEASE SEE PAGE 62.

KEEPING OUR COOL

SOLUTIONS TO GLOBAL WARMING

Like many playgrounds, the one at Spirit Lake Elementary School in Spirit Lake, Iowa, has swings, slides, and climbing bars. What makes this playground stand out are the two huge poles in the field behind it. One is about 14 stories tall; the other is even taller. At the top of each pole is what looks like a giant airplane propeller. These machines are called wind turbines.

Arms outstretched, a girl mimics the turbines that capture the clean power of the wind. Switching to carbon-free energy sources is one way we can help put the brakes on global warming.

When the wind blows—and it blows a lot across the Iowa plains—it spins a turbine's propellers, or blades. The spinning blades turn a gear in a box inside the pole. This generates electricity. The smaller turbine provides all the electricity the elementary school needs. The larger turbine powers Spirit Lake's middle school and high school, the bus barn, the football stadium lights, and more. In fact, the big turbine generates more electricity than the schools need. The extra electricity is sold to the local utility company, earning the schools about $120,000 a year. That's sweet. Even sweeter is the fact that the Spirit Lake schools are powered without producing one bit of greenhouse gas.

There's no quick and easy way to fix global warming. The Spirit Lake schools on their own can barely dent the problem of Earth's changing climate. But if we all work together and do our part to reduce the amount of carbon dioxide and other greenhouse gases going into the air, we may be able to keep our planet cooler in the future. To do so, we have to rethink the way we produce and use energy.

Most people still depend on fossil fuels for the energy we need to heat and cool our homes and schools, to power our lights and computers, to run our factories, and to make our cars and airplanes go. Much of the world's electricity comes from coal-burning power plants. If we keep burning fossil fuels at the current pace of growth, however, climate scientists predict that the extra carbon released into the atmosphere could cause global temperatures to climb by more than 11 degrees Fahrenheit (6 degrees Celsius) by 2100. That really would put Earth in the hot seat—and it could be a disaster for a great deal of life on our planet.

Sound scary? It is. But the good news is that it doesn't have to happen. Scientists believe we can limit the most severe consequences of climate change if we slash back our use of fossil fuels, starting right now.

Where can our energy-hungry society turn to replace fossil fuels? As students in Spirit Lake know, one solution is blowing in the wind. Today more and more people around the planet are harnessing the breeze to generate electricity. From California to Brazil to Spain to India to China, wind farms consisting of dozens or even hundreds of giant turbines already provide millions of people with power. More turbines are going up every day. Industry experts predict that wind power could provide up to one-third or

A girl demonstrates a bright idea—using sunlight to generate electricity.

more of the world's electricity by 2050.

Solar energy use is also growing by leaps and bounds. You've probably seen solar panels, also called photovoltaic cells, on the rooftops of some houses and buildings. These panels convert sunlight into electricity that directly powers a building's lights and appliances. Solar farms—also called solar thermal power plants—operate on a much larger scale. Often located in deserts, they consist of acres and acres of huge rows of solar panels, which concentrate the sun's heat to drive steam turbines that generate electricity. This electricity feeds straight into the power grid, which then delivers it to customers. The biggest solar farms can supply electricity for 30,000 homes.

Wind and solar power are called renewable energy sources because we don't have to worry about running out of them—the wind is always blowing and the sun is always shining somewhere. Fossil fuels, on the other hand, are not renewable. When they're used up, that's it.

Stretching longer than a football field, this "sea snake" is nothing to be afraid of. Nicknamed for its long, tubular shape, it's a machine that uses the motion of the ocean to generate electricity. It's part of the world's first commercial wave-energy farm, which opened off the north coast of Portugal in the fall of 2008.

Other clean, renewable sources of electricity include hydropower, geothermal energy, and biomass. Hydropower uses moving water—from rivers, dams, and even ocean waves—to generate electricity. Geothermal energy comes from hot rocks and fluids beneath Earth's surface. The underground steam and hot water can be tapped to heat buildings directly or to generate electricity in power plants. Biomass power comes from stuff we often think of as garbage: dead trees, yard clippings, sawdust, leftover crops, and even animal manure. These things can be burned at special power plants to drive steam turbines that produce electricity.

Some experts believe that expanding our use of nuclear power, which emits no greenhouse gases, would be the fastest way to put the brakes on global warming. Nuclear power already provides about 20 percent of the

Renewable energy rocks! Water roaring through a dam in Arizona generates electricity at a power plant below the dam (top). In Iceland, swimmers enjoy a lake warmed by hot water piped up from underground, which also fuels the geothermal power plant behind the lake (center). Last up: cow power. The methane gas naturally released by cow manure can be captured and used to power electric generators.

electricity used by Americans and 78 percent of France's electricity. Building new nuclear power plants is very expensive, however, and many people are concerned about the storage of radioactive nuclear waste and the possibility of accidents such as nuclear meltdowns.

Renewable energy sources aren't perfect either. Solar plants and wind farms both take up a lot of land area. Some people think wind turbines are ugly, and they don't like the noise they make. Also, the rotating blades can kill birds and bats—though a lot more of these animals fall victim to cats, cars, and collisions with high-rise buildings. But on the whole, the advantages of renewable energy technologies outweigh the drawbacks. So why isn't everyone switching to them? A big reason is that right now it's still cheaper to make energy from fossil fuels. Rapid advances in technology, however, are fast making wind, solar, and other alternative energies increasingly practical, efficient, and affordable.

Researchers are also developing ways to capture the carbon dioxide created by coal-burning power plants and store it safely deep underground, where it can't escape into the atmosphere. Trials of this process, called carbon sequestration, are underway in Australia, Norway, and several other countries. Bright minds around the world are also working on ways to take the carbon out of transportation. Vehicles that run on special fuel cells are being tested. The hope is that someday we'll be able to charge our electric cars with renewable wind or sun or wave energy—no fossil fuels involved. In the meantime, more and more carmakers are concentrating on making today's gas-powered autos more fuel-efficient.

Experts say that one of the most effective ways to help curb global warming is to make our transportation, buildings, and appliances more energy-efficient, so that they use less power in the first place. Just by improving energy efficiency—using today's technological know-how—we could cut greenhouse gas emissions by a third. "It wouldn't solve the problem," says Daniel Sosland, director of Environment Northeast, a nonprofit environmental research group. "But it's the cheapest first step. And you have to do it to be on the right path." We've already taken a few steps down this path. New refrigerators, for example, consume 70 percent less energy than those made 40 years ago. Creative design—and plenty of insulation—is reducing the amount of fuel needed to heat and cool new buildings.

Even if everyone stopped producing greenhouse gases this very minute, climate scientists predict that Earth will still keep warming up by another degree or two Fahrenheit. That's got lots of people thinking about how to adapt to the changes this would bring, such as rising sea levels. Architects in low-lying Holland, for instance, have designed houses that float with the water level.

There's no doubt that climate change presents a great challenge to people around the planet. It's also an exciting opportunity for innovation. Solar, wind, and other renewable energy projects are already creating new business opportunities and lots of jobs. Now is the time for all of us—communities, companies, governments, and yes, you and me—to get involved. What we do from this day forward will have a big effect on what our world is like in the future.

Designed by students at the University of Maryland, this house is completely powered by the sun. The team's inspiration came from what they call "the ultimate solar collector," the leaf.

CLIMATE CONNECTIONS

 npr® npr.org NATIONAL GEOGRAPHIC

FROM CACAO BEAN TO CHOCOLATE

How Chocolate Can Save the Planet

THERE ARE LOTS of reasons to love chocolate, but how can it help with global climate change? The answer can be found in a patch of rain forest in eastern Brazil. Farmers there are being encouraged to grow cacao trees—the source of chocolate—under the canopy of larger rain forest trees, a method called cabruca. And here's the climate connection: Rain forest trees and plants store massive amounts of carbon, which keeps it from getting into the air as carbon dioxide. All too often, rain forests are destroyed for wood and to create fields for pasture and crops. The cabruca method of raising chocolate enables farmers to make a profit and to preserve part of the rain forest. By itself this won't fix Earth's climate problem, but it may help a little. And at least we'll have more chocolate.

— Adapted from Climate Connections report, ©2007, NPR®. All Rights Reserved.

HUMAN FOOTPRINT.

Everything you eat. Everything you drink. Everything you use. Your entire life's consumption. In one place at one time.

How many canned sodas does the average American drink in a lifetime? The answer is spelled out here with soda cans: **43,371.** If all these cans were lined up side by side, they would stretch for **3.42** miles. That's **43,371** opportunities to recycle!

GREEN GUIDE

HOT TIPS TO FIGHT GLOBAL WARMING

Share these energy-saving tips with your parents!

- Wash your clothes in cold water instead of hot. Washing machines produce over 500 pounds of CO_2 a year when run on hot water. Your clothes will be just as clean and may even last longer when laundered in cold water.

- Whenever possible, dry your clothes on a line outside or a rack indoors. Dryers produce about 1,450 pounds of CO_2 per year.

- Run your dishwasher only when full, and always set it to the energy saver mode.

EARTH'S VOICES

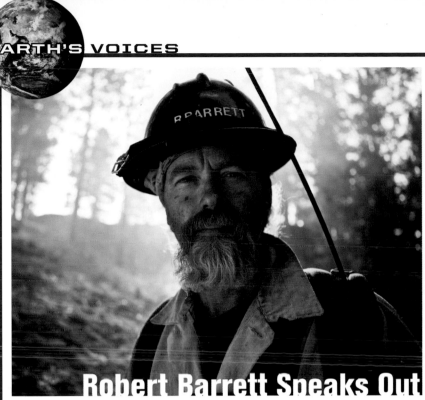

Robert Barrett Speaks Out

Robert Barrett is a professional firefighter who specializes in fighting wildfires. He lives in Pocatello, Idaho.

What is your favorite place on Earth?
A little piece of mountain property just outside of Pocatello, Idaho. Mule deer, moose, and a variety of other animals enjoy it as well. It is a great place to listen to the wind and the birds and enjoy nature.

What advice do you have for kids about reversing global warming?
Learn as much as you can about global warming. Be a leader and show your friends, brothers, and sisters how cool it is to care about the Earth. Get together with friends and encourage them to ride bikes or walk to school. Every once in a while pay attention to those doggone boring news shows and those silly politicians and see if you can tell who might be serious about helping the environment.

Have you ever seen global warming at work?
As a wildland firefighter, I have spent most of the last two decades working with Hotshots, firefighting crews that specialize in the hottest parts of wildfires. I have traveled all over the country, including Alaska, fighting the big fires and assisting with initial attack on small fires. Rangelands and forests are burning out of control more frequently and growing larger than we ever imagined just a few short years ago. While other factors are involved, I believe that global warming has played a significant role in this increase in large fire activity.

What is your favorite animal?
The mountain lion. Once I came face to face with one when I tumbled off a short cliff while scouting on a large fire in central Utah. The fire was starting to make a run and the lion and I were in the process of moving fast to get out of the way of the oncoming flames. The meeting barely lasted a half second but made quite an impression.

The world would be a better place if...
We all paid more attention to each other than to the television.

Thirty-six percent of Americans drink bottled water every day, compared to 72% of Germans and 56% of Mexicans. Japanese (21%), Australians (19%), and British (16%) are the least likely to drink bottled water daily.

SIX°DEGREES
COULD CHANGE THE WORLD

4 IF GLOBAL WARMING GOES UNCHECKED AND THE EARTH WARMS **DEGREES CELSIUS** (7.2 Degrees Fahrenheit):

- Rising oceans could take over coastal cities such as Alexandria in Egypt, Shanghai in China, and Boston in the U.S.

- The disappearance of glaciers may deprive many of Earth's inhabitants of freshwater.

- Throughout the world, snowfall could be rare except at the highest altitudes.

- A part of Antarctica could collapse, causing sea levels to rise even more.

- On the positive side, northern Canada's agriculture could boom, and a Scandinavian beach could be the next tourism hotspot.

6
5
4
3
2
1

You don't have to climb out on a limb to help protect our planet, but as these kids show, it can be fun! Playing outdoors, instead of staying inside and using electricity to play video games, is just one of the ways you can help reduce the amount of heat-trapping greenhouse gases released into the air.

WHAT YOU DO COUNTS

PROTECTING OUR PLANET

Tackling global warming isn't just about building giant wind turbines and solar farms. We all have a role to play in bringing Earth's changing climate under control. What you do counts.

So go fly a kite. Take a walk. Kick a ball. Climb a tree. Look at the stars! Having fun outdoors—instead of staying inside and watching TV—is one way you can shrink the amount of carbon dioxide that's produced when you use energy that comes from burning fossil fuels. That's called your carbon footprint. Lots of everyday activities contribute to a person's carbon footprint, including flipping on a light, riding in a car or bus, and even taking a bath. It takes energy, after all, to warm the water and to move it through the pipes to the tub.

Every year, each American on average adds more than 40,000 pounds of carbon dioxide to the air. To get an idea of just how much this is, think of CO_2 as an inflated balloon. One pound of the heat-trapping gas would fill a balloon as wide as a hula hoop—about two and a half feet. Forty thousand of these one-pound carbon dioxide balloons would fill four Olympic-size swimming pools. That's quite a footprint.

By making smart choices about how you use energy, however, you can reduce your own carbon footprint and help protect our planet. It's called going green, and you don't need complicated new technology to do this, just new behavior. Consider the people of Juneau, Alaska. In the spring of 2008, they slashed back their use of electricity by more than 30 percent in only a few weeks, just by changing their energy habits. They started hanging their laundry outside to dry instead of using power-hogging electric dryers, for example, and they piled on extra blankets to stay warm instead of cranking up the heat. They replaced regular incandescent lightbulbs with energy-smart compact fluorescent lamps (CFLs), and they only turned on the lights when they really, really needed to.

Were Juneau's residents seized by a sudden urge to go green and save the Earth? Well, no. In this case they just wanted to save the green stuff—money, that is. A series of avalanches had knocked out the city's connection to

It's not a pretty picture. Each of the balloons above represents one pound of carbon dioxide. Burning one gallon of gasoline in an automobile spews about 19 pounds of CO_2 into the air. Just producing that gasoline from oil in the first place created 6 pounds of CO_2. That adds up to a grand total of 25—count them—balloons of CO_2 for every gallon of gas we burn.

the hydroelectric power plant, and the price of electricity had quadrupled overnight. People were trying to keep their electric bills from skyrocketing. But no matter the reason, Juneau's lesson is that if we really want to save energy, we can make it happen.

Reducing the amount of energy you use in the first place is the easiest way to shrink your carbon footprint and make a difference right away. So think twice before you flip a switch. Unless your electricity comes from a clean energy source, every time you turn on a lamp or appliance, a power plant could be burning fossil fuels, which emit greenhouse gases that cause global warming. Don't forget to turn things off when you're through with them. Wasted electricity just sends more CO_2 into the sky. Speaking

By replacing just one regular lightbulb with a CFL, you can reduce CO$_2$ emissions by an amount equal to that released by burning this 500-pound pile of coal.

of wasting electricity, that's what incandescent lightbulbs do, compared to CFLs. CFLs use only about a quarter of the power and last up to ten times longer. No wonder people in Juneau changed to them. And no wonder they wore heavy sweaters and thick socks to help keep away the chill: Heating a house consumes huge amounts of energy. So does cooling one with air-conditioning in the summer.

Energy experts estimate that as much as five to eight percent of U.S. household electricity is wasted by vampires. Vampires? That's what they call appliances that keep sucking up power as long as they're plugged in, even when you've turned them off. Televisions, video game players, microwaves, computers, and many other electronic gadgets are vampires. So are chargers for cell phones and music players. So unplug chargers from the wall when you're finished with them. And talk to your parents about plugging electronics into a power strip that can be turned off at the source when the equipment isn't in use. These two easy steps will help save money on your family's electric bill and cut back your carbon footprint.

Every gallon of gasoline burned in a car adds a little more than 25 pounds of CO$_2$ to the atmosphere. That can add up to a big chunk of your carbon footprint. So the less you and your family use a car, the better. Ride your bike or walk wherever and whenever you can. If you live too far from school to get there with your own two legs, take the bus or carpool. Both are more fuel-efficient than going solo. When you do ride in the car, encourage your parents to turn it off rather than letting it idle while you wait in it for more than a minute or so. An idling engine gobbles more gas and spews out more CO$_2$ than just restarting your car. And gas is too expensive to waste—just ask a grown-up.

Another simple way to reduce your energy consumption is to buy less stuff. That's because making new things uses energy. Practically every item you can purchase requires fuel to produce it, package it, transport it, and

eventually get rid of it. So before you buy something, think hard about whether you really need it. You'll often decide it isn't worth all that energy. Also think about where things come from. Food that is grown locally, for example, takes less fuel to get to us than food shipped from thousands of miles away. If you're lucky enough to have a farmers market nearby, ask your parents to shop there for fresh food. Even better, try growing your own vegetables and fruit if you have the space.

Reusing and recycling items will also help cut back your carbon footprint. Pass along clothes you've outgrown or toys you no longer play with to family and friends, or donate them to charities. Fill your own reusable water bottle from the tap instead of buying water in plastic bottles. To produce and ship all those plastic water bottles consumes huge amounts of fossil fuels. Recycle everything you can, especially glass bottles, aluminum cans, and plastic and paper items. It usually takes less energy to recycle these things than to make new ones. If we all practice the three Rs—reduce, reuse, and recycle—it can make a big difference in the health of our planet.

Besides decreasing the amount of greenhouse gases you release into the

A delicious way to go green is to buy your greens and other fresh foods at a farmers market, as these shoppers in Croatia are doing. Part of the fun is meeting the people who grow the food you're buying.

atmosphere, how else can you limit climate change? Plant stuff! It's fun, and the more trees, shrubs, and other plants there are to soak up carbon dioxide, the better. Dr. Wangari Maathai, an environmentalist who won the Nobel Peace Prize in 2004, founded the Greenbelt Movement in Kenya, which focuses on planting trees. She says, "Every one of us needs ten trees in our life. Ten, to take care of your own carbon dioxide. Go plant your own ten trees. Don't use other people's trees." Now, planting your own trees won't stop global warming all by itself, but it's another important step in the right direction.

Planting a tree today can help Earth stay cooler in the future. That's something to smile about! As a tree grows, it traps more and more carbon dioxide every year.

So is encouraging policymakers to save the world's forests. Write letters, send emails—let people know you are concerned about climate change. It's your future, and you have more influence than you might think. You can lobby your local government to build more sidewalks and bike lanes to make it safer and easier for people to reduce their car use. You can start recycling drives at your school. James Peterson, a student at George Mason High School in Falls Church, Virginia, talked school officials into installing solar power at the school and then led the fund-raising drive to put the panels in place. "I wanted to educate the community and the students about alternative energies and how they are viable," he said.

If you really want to make a difference, think about pursuing a career in environmental science or renewable energy. You might invent new, clean ways to generate electricity or power transportation, make alternative energy more efficient, or find ways to protect wildlife from the effects of global warming. Whatever you do, stay involved and aware. As Sylvia Earle, an oceanographer who studies the effect of climate change on the seas, says, "The next ten years may be the most important in all of the future of humankind. So use the power that you have, whoever you are, whatever it is you do. The world needs what you've got to give."

Pedal power propels a family through Redwood National Park in California, just one of the many extraordinary places on our planet. It's a wonderful world. What we do now can help it stay that way in the future.

CLIMATE CONNECTIONS

npr.org

NATIONAL GEOGRAPHIC

A PLANE LANDS AT RUSH HOUR.

What's Greener, Flying or Driving?

MANY PEOPLE WANT TO KNOW how much greenhouse gas is poured into the atmosphere by commercial flights. Experts say that aircraft are a small but significant source of the warming gases created by humans, accounting for about 3 percent of the world's total emissions. A typical airliner flying across the United States produces close to three tons of carbon dioxide per passenger. So would it be better to take that cross-country trip by car? Not according to the experts. They say you will roughly double your emissions if you decide to drive. Take the train, however, and you can cut your carbon footprint in half.

— *Adapted from Climate Connections report, ©2007, NPR®. All Rights Reserved.*

HUMAN FOOTPRINT

Everything you eat. Everything you drink. Everything you use. Your entire life's consumption. In one place at one time.

Whether baked, mashed, or fried, potatoes are a favorite food. The average American consumes **28,800** of them in a lifetime. That equals **13,924** pounds, or **6.96** tons, of potatoes per person. Buying locally grown potatoes and other food will help trim your carbon footprint.

GREEN GUIDE

HOT TIPS TO FIGHT GLOBAL WARMING

Share these energy-saving tips with your parents!

- Replace at least five incandescent lightbulbs in your home with compact fluorescents.

- Turn off your TV, DVD player, computer, and cable box. Even in "standby" mode, your home entertainment center and computer consume energy. Plug them into a power strip and turn it off after you shut down your electronics.

- Eat foods grown locally. When your produce doesn't have to travel as far to the dinner table, it reduces the carbon emissions that are spewn in transit.

EARTH'S VOICES

David de Rothschild Speaks Out

David de Rothschild is a British environmentalist and former National Geographic Emerging Explorer, as well as the founder of Adventure Ecology, an organization dedicated to spreading the word about global warming and other environmental concerns.

What is your favorite place on Earth?
Hickory Bay, New Zealand.

What advice do you have for kids about reversing global warming?
It's our everyday human activities that have created the problems we are now experiencing, therefore we are the ones who hold the keys to the solutions. And the first stepping-stone to any solution is to remain optimistic and start acting.

Have you ever seen global warming at work?
In early 2006, I spent three months traveling across the Arctic Ocean, which sadly allowed me to experience global warming firsthand. I was about three days' travel from the North Pole, whereby I should have been shivering away in my tent. However, due to abnormally warm weather, I was sweating. If anyone tells you global warming is not happening, they are wrong—it is!

What is your favorite animal?
The bearded pig!

What do you do to help stop global warming?
I work hard to tell stories and promote the issues in a way that I hope helps to inspire a greater understanding and ultimately respect for our planet and its well-being.

How big is your carbon footprint?
Bigger than average, but it's not as big as it could be! I work hard to tread as lightly as I can, and then I offset.

The world would be a better place if ...
We could all be a little more curious.

What's one thing you wish kids knew about global warming?
There are big challenges ahead but it's not all bad news! The power to stop global warming lies in our hands, and right now we are living in a time when there are currently more solutions than there are problems!

SIX DEGREES COULD CHANGE THE WORLD

5 IF GLOBAL WARMING GOES UNCHECKED AND THE EARTH WARMS **DEGREES CELSIUS** (9 Degrees Fahrenheit):

- Earth's atmosphere would become increasingly poisonous. The planet's rain forests will have burned up and disappeared completely.

- The remaining ice sheets would have vanished from both poles, and rising seas will begin to penetrate far into continental interiors. Increasing areas of the planet would become uninhabitable, and people would flock to areas that could still support life, such as northern Canada and the Antarctic.

- Food and freshwater will become increasingly rare. The poor would likely suffer the most.

6 IF GLOBAL WARMING GOES UNCHECKED AND THE EARTH WARMS **DEGREES CELSIUS** (10.8 Degrees Fahrenheit):

- The oceans would become mostly lifeless, the deserts could march across continents, and natural disasters such as super hurricanes could become common events.

- Many species of life on Earth could die out.

FOR MORE INFORMATION ABOUT THESE ▢ NATIONAL GEOGRAPHIC INITIATIVES, PLEASE SEE PAGE 62.

Here are some great sources to help you learn more about climate change and ways you can help protect our planet. Those with an asterisk (*) were created especially for young people.

BOOKS

Braasch, Gary. *Earth Under Fire: How Global Warming is Changing the World.* University of California Press, 2007. Features awesome photographs.

*Cherry, Lynne, and Gary Braasch. *How We Know What We Know About Our Changing Climate: Scientists and Kids Explore Global Warming.* Dawn Publications, 2008. Focuses on how scientists are researching climate change and its effects.

*David, Laurie, and Cambria Gordon. *The Down-to-Earth Guide to Global Warming.* Scholastic, 2007. Fact-packed and fun to read, with lots of ideas on how kids can get involved.

*Gore, Al. *An Inconvenient Truth: The Crisis of Global Warming.* Viking, 2007. A book for young readers based on the Academy Award-winning film, "An Inconvenient Truth."

*Johnson, Kirk, and Mary Ann Bonnell. *Gas Trees and Car Turds: A Kids' Guide to the Roots of Global Warming.* Fulcrum Publishing, 2007. An entertaining introduction to the carbon cycle and global warming.

*McKay, Kim, and Jenny Bonnin. *True Green for Kids: 100 Things You Can Do to Save the Planet.* National Geographic, 2008. Filled with 100 fun and practical ways to make the world a greener place.

*Rockwell, Anne. *Why Are the Ice Caps Melting? The Dangers of Global Warming.* Collins, 2006. A very simple introduction to global warming.

de Rothschild, David. *The Live Earth Global Warming Survival Handbook: 77 Essential Skills to Stop Climate Change.* Rodale Books, 2007. Lots of useful tips, presented in a clever survival guide form.

WEB SITES

*Adventure Ecology. adventureecology.org A mixture of adventure, education, creative arts, and planet-friendly lifestyle tips. Click on links to travel the world as an "eco-adventurer."

The Daily Climate thedailyclimate.com News feeds on climate change from major media outlets.

*Energy Information Administration Kid's Page. eia.doe.gov/kids Energy facts, energy history, glossary of energy terms, and riddles, puzzles, and games.

ENERGY STAR Program energystar.gov Info on energy-saving appliances and more.

*EPA Climate Change Kids Page epa.gov/climatechange/kids Games, links, animations, and climate change info from the U.S. Environmental Protection Agency.

NASA Goddard Institute for Space Studies giss.nasa.gov A terrific source of news releases, research, and reports about climate change.

National Geographic Preserve Our Planet nationalgeographic.com/ preserveourplanet This site has links to a wide variety of information about climate change. You can take a global warming quiz, view maps displaying the impact of climate change around the globe, see videos about the environment, and more.

National Renewable Energy Laboratory (NREL) nrel.gov America's primary laboratory for renewable energy research.

*National Resources Defense Council's Green Squad nrdc.org/greensquad Tips for making your school healthier for you and the environment.

*Nickelodeon The Big Green Help nick.com/biggreenhelp Lively site with games, videos, and tips on saving energy.

Personal Emissions Calculator epa.gov/climatechange/emissions/ ind_calculator.html Calculte your carbon footprint and learn how you can reduce it.

*Pew Center on Global Climate Change. Global Warming—Kids Page Basic information and links to other kid-friendly sites, including one in India. pewclimate.org/global-warming-basics/kidspage.cfm

RealClimate realclimate.org Informative blog on climate science by working climate scientists.

Scripps CO_2 Program scrippsco2.ucsd.edu Learn more about carbon dioxide, Charles David Keeling, and the Keeling curve at this site.

U.S. Department of Energy Solar Decathlon solardecathlon.org Held every two years, the Solar Decathlon joins 20 college and university teams in a competition to design, build, and operate the most attractive and energy-efficient solar-powered house. At this site you can see the winners of past decathlons and learn about upcoming events. The next decathlon is scheduled for the fall of 2009 in Washington, D.C.

World Wildlife Fund worldwildlife.org/climate/ whatyoucando.html Lots of useful tips on how individuals, families, and communities can help slow climate change. There's even a section on how to "green your backpack."

VIDEOS

National Geographic Video Click "Environment" to watch videos on global warming, going green, energy, and other topics. video.nationalgeographic.com/ video/index.html

I consulted many sources for this book. These are the ones I found most useful or interesting.

BOOKS

Flannery, Tim. *The Weather Makers: How Man Is Changing the Climate and What It Means for Life on Earth.* Atlantic Monthly Press, 2005.

Kolbert, Elizabeth. *Field Notes from a Catastrophe: Man, Nature, and Climate Change.* Bloomsbury, 2006.

Lomborg, Bjorn. *Cool It: The Skeptical Environmentalist's Guide to Global Warming.* Knopf, 2007.

Lynas, Mark. *Six Degrees: Our Future on a Hotter Planet.* National Geographic, 2008.

McKay, Kim, and Jenny Bonnin. *True Green: 100 Everyday Ways You Can Contribute to a Healthier Planet.* National Geographic, 2006.

Weiner, Jonathan. *The Next One Hundred Years: Shaping the Fate of Our Living Earth.* Bantam Books, 1990.

MAGAZINES

The Green Guide. Spring 2008.
National Geographic. Changing Climate Special Report, 2008.
National Geographic. Global Warming Issue, September 2004.
New York Times Magazine. The Green Issue, April 20, 2008.

ARTICLES AND REPORTS

Appenzeller, Tim. "The Big Thaw." *National Geographic,* June 2007.

Bryant Park Project. "After Avalanche, Juneau Races to Conserve Power." NPR, April 30, 2008. www.npr.org/templates/story/story.php?storyId=90060569

Chadwick, Douglas H. "Crown of the Continent." *National Geographic,* Sept. 2007.

Chandler, Michael Alison. "Leading by Example," *Washington Post,* Fairfax Extra, July 17, 2008.

CSIRO Australia. "Ocean Life Under Threat From Climate Change." *ScienceDaily* June 11, 2008. www.sciencedaily.com/releases/2008/06/080606105448.htm

Dybas, Cheryl. "Winter Ice on Lakes, Rivers, Ponds: A Thing of the Past?" National Science Foundation Publication, June 10, 2008. www.nsf.gov/discoveries/disc_summ.jsp?cntn_id=110967

Eilperin, Juliet. "Carbon Output Must Near Zero to Avert Danger, New Studies Say." *Washington Post,* March 10, 2008.

Handwerk, Brian. "Frog Extinctions Linked to Global Warming." *National Geographic News,* Jan. 12, 2006. news.nationalgeographic.com/news/2006/01/0112_060112_frog_climate.html

Hoag, Hannah. "Global Warming Already Causing Extinctions, Scientists Say." *National Geographic News,* Nov. 28, 2006. news.nationalgeographic.com/news/2006/11/061128-global-warming.html

Holland, Jennifer S. "Acid Threat." *National Geographic,* Nov. 2007.

Intergovernmental Panel on Climate Change. "Climate Change 2007: Synthesis Report. Summary for Policymakers." www.ipcc.ch/pdf/assessment-report/ar4/syr/ar4_syr_spm.pdf

Jensen, Olaf P., et.al. "Spatial analysis of ice phenology trends across the Laurentian Great Lakes region during a recent warming period." *Limnology & Oceanography,* 52(5), 2007, pp. 2013-2026.

National Museum of Natural History. "Scientists at the Smithsonian's National Museum of Natural History Find Global Warming to be Major Factor in Early Blossoming Flowers in Washington." www.mnh.si.edu/highlight/spring00/spring00_feature.html

National Science Foundation. "Climate Change Drives Widespread Amphibian Extinctions." Press Release 06-008, Jan. 11, 2006. www.nsf.gov/news/news_summ.jsp?cntn_id=105707

Norris, Scott. "Hibernating Animals Suffer Dangerous Wakeup Calls Due to Warming." *National Geographic News,* February 2, 2007. news.nationalgeographic.com/news/2007/02/070202-groundhog_2.html

Pamperin, Nathan. J., et. al. "Interspecific Killing of an Arctic Fox by a Red Fox at Prudhoe Bay, Alaska." *Arctic* 59 (4) (December 2006), pp. 361-364. pubs.aina.ucalgary.ca/arctic/Arctic59-4-361.pdf

Roig-Franzia, Manuel. "Panama Hotel is Imperiled Frogs' Lifeboat." *Washington Post,* Oct. 26, 2006.

Ryan, John. "Juneau Goes Into Conservation Overdrive." NPR, All Things Considered, May 2, 2008. www.npr.org/templates/story/story.php?storyId=90142720

Ryan, John. "With Juneau's Power Restored, Conservation Drops." NPR, Morning Edition, Aug. 15, 2008. www.npr.org/templates/story/story.php?storyId=93619395

Sasso, Anne. "Mountain Messengers." Smithsonian.com, January 28, 2008. www.smithsonianmag.com/specialsections/ecocenter/Mountain_Messengers.html?c=y&page=1

"Scientific Assessment of the Effects of Global Change on the United States: A Report of the Committee on Environment and Natural Resources National Science and Technology Council." May 2008. www.climatescience.gov/Library/scientific-assessment/

Scripps Institution of Oceanography. "Biography of Charles David Keeling." scrippsco2.ucsd.edu/sub_program_history/charles_david_keeling_biography.html

Struck, Doug. "A Big Drop in Emissions is Possible with Today's Technology." *Washington Post,* Jan. 21, 2008.

Tannerfeldt, Magnus. "The Arctic Fox, Alopex lagopus." SEFALO, Stockholm University. www.zoologi.su.se/research/alopex/the_arctic_fox.htm

Tremlett, Giles, and Paul Hamilos. "Portugal Gambles on Sea Snakes Providing an Energy Boost." *The Guardian,* October 1, 2007. www.guardian.co.uk/environment/2007/oct/01/waveandtidalpower.renewableenergy

SELECT BIBLIOGRAPHY (CONT.)

University of Texas at Austin. "Chasing butterflies leads biologist to illuminate global warming trend." Profile of Camille Parmesan. www.utexas.edu/research/profiles/parmesan.html

U.S. Geological Survey. "Future Retreat of Arctic Sea Ice Will Lower Polar Bear Populations and Limit Their Distribution." 9/7/2007 release. www.usgs.gov/newsroom/article.asp?ID=1773

Vidal, John. "World's Biggest Solar Farm at Centre of Portugal's Ambitious Energy Plan." The Guardian, June 6, 2008. www.guardian.co.uk/environment/2008/jun/06/renewableenergy.alternativeenergy

VIDEOS
"Iowa Wind Power" and "Turning Point: State of the Earth." National Geographic Video. video.nationalgeographic.com

WEB SITES
Climate Connections. National Public Radio and National Geographic npr.org/climateconnections

Energy Story, California Energy Commission energyquest.ca.gov/story/index.html#table

Forces of Change: Arctic Smithsonian/National Museum of Natural History forces.si.edu/index.html

Intergovernmental Panel on Climate Change (IPCC) www.ipcc.ch

National Geographic Global Warming science.nationalgeographic.com/science/environment/global-warming/
National Geographic Green Guide thegreenguide.com

National Geographic Preserve Our Planet nationalgeographic.com/preserveourplanet

National Oceanic and Atmospheric Administration. Arctic Change arctic.noaa.gov/detect

National Snow and Ice Education Center nsidc.org/cryosphere

Union of Concerned Scientists Global Warming ucsusa.org/global_warming

U.S. Climate Change Science Program climatescience.gov/default.php

U.S. Department of Energy. Energy Efficiency and Renewable Energy eere.energy.gov

U.S. National Park Service Glacier National Park nps.gov/glac

BULLETIN SOURCES
Features in the Bulletin sections were closely adapted from the following:

CLIMATE CONNECTIONS
Climate Connections is a special broadcast on National Public Radio (NPR) that is produced in partnership with National Geographic. It features stories from around the globe that explore how climate is shaping people and people are shaping the climate. You can listen to the original reports or read them on NPR.org. The Climate Connections section also features photos, maps, and links to other sites having to do with climate change. http://www.npr.org/templates/story/story.php?storyId=9657621

PENGUINS HELPED AND HURT BY CHANGING CLIMATE
©2008, NPR®, News report by NPR's Daniel Zwerdling was originally broadcast on NPR's All Things Considered® on March 31, 2008, and is used as an adaptation with the permission of NPR. Any unauthorized duplication is strictly prohibited.

SHALLOW WATER AHEAD FOR PANAMA CANAL
©2008, NPR®, News report by NPR's Jon Hamilton was originally broadcast on NPR's Morning Edition® on March 3, 2008, and is used as an adaptation with the permission of NPR. Any unauthorized duplication is strictly prohibited.

DROUGHT FORCES DESERT NOMADS TO SETTLE DOWN
©2007, NPR®, News report by NPR's Richard Harris was originally broadcast on NPR's Morning Edition® on July 2, 2007, and is used as an adaptation with the permission of NPR. Any unauthorized duplication is strictly prohibited.

HOW CHOCOLATE CAN SAVE THE PLANET
©2007, NPR®, News report by NPR's Joanne Silberner was originally

broadcast on NPR's Morning Edition® on November 19, 2007, and is used as an adaptation with the permission of NPR. Any unauthorized duplication is strictly prohibited.

WHAT'S GREENER, FLYING OR DRIVING?
©2007, NPR®, News report was originally broadcast on NPR's Morning Edition® on October 11, 2007, and is used as an adaptation with the permission of NPR. Any unauthorized duplication is strictly prohibited.

GREEN GUIDE
Many of the "Green Tips" in the Bulletin spreads were adapted from the Green Guide, a National Geographic Web site and magazine devoted 100 percent to making living in an environmentally-aware way easy, understandable and practical. thegreenguide.com/
A Green Guide radio segment with editor Seth Bauer is online at www.NGWeekend.com.

GREENDEX
Sponsored by National Geographic and Globescan, Greendex is a research project that tracks the behavior of people in countries around the globe on such issues as energy use, conservation, transportation choices, and food sources. You can take a quiz and also calculate your own "Greendex" and see how it compares with that of people in other countries. www.nationalgeographic.com/greendex

HUMAN FOOTPRINT
This National Geographic film shows what an average American consumes—and discards—in a lifetime, all in one place at one time via a series of dramatic, revealing and informative visual demonstrations. The Human Footprint Web site has a fun "consumption interactive" that lets you compare your footprint with that of others. channel.nationalgeographic.com/channel/human-footprint/

SIX DEGREES COULD CHANGE THE WORLD
This National Geographic film leads a degree-by-degree journey to explore what each rising—and critical—degree could mean for the future of our people and planet. Through powerful filmmaking and intimate profiles, this special illustrates how global warming has already affected the reefs of Australia, the ice fields of Greenland, and the Amazonian rain forest. With a sobering look at the effects of our world's insatiable appetite for energy, *Six Degrees Could Change the World* explains what's real, what's still controversial, and how existing technologies and remedies could help dial back the global thermometer. The film is a companion to the book *Six Degrees: Our Future on a Hotter Planet,* by Mark Lynas.

QUOTE SOURCES
Quotations were taken from the following sources, which are fully cited on pages 60-62:

Page 10: "It will be the first time..." *National Geographic* magazine (NGM) 6/07; Page 10: "Things that normally..." NGM 9/04; Page 11: "When I go..." NGM 6/07; Page 13: "The melt..." NGM 7/06; Page 20: "two big..." *The Next One Hundred Years,* p.21; Page 23: "We humans..." *National Geographic Climate Change Special Report* (NGCCSR); Page 32: "Disease is..." National Geographic News (NG News), 1/12/06; Page 32: "We're seeing..." NGCCSR; Page 33: "When they..." NG News, 2/2/07; Page 33: "What surprises me..." NG News, 11/28/06; Page 46: "It wouldn't solve..." *Washington Post,* 1/1/08; Page 56: "Everyone of us..." National Geographic, *Turning Point, State of the Earth* video; Page 56: "I wanted to educate..." *Washington Post,* 7/17/08; Page 56: "The next ten years..." NG, Final Report, *State of the Earth* video.

INDEX

PHOTO CREDITS

Ami Vitale: 2-3; **Corbis:** Ashley Cooper: 27; Remi Benali: 26 top; Hans Georg Roth: 55; Scott McDermott: 59 bottom; NASA: 1, 17 top, 29 top, 39 top, 49 top, 59 top; NOAA: 26 bottom; Scott T. Smith: 32; Chase Swift: 15; LWA-Dann Tardif: 13; **Frans Lanting:** 17 bottom; **Getty Images:** Frans Lemmens/Photographer's Choice: 38 top; Photodisc Red: 56; Stuart Redler/ Photonica: 50-51; Chris Sattlberger/ The Image Bank: 58 top; David Stubbs/Aurora: 57; **iStockPhoto:** Back Cover; Eva Serrabassa: 40-41; Mark Wagg: 48 top; **Matthias Clamer:** 52-53; **Minden Pictures:** Pete Oxford: 30-31; **NGM:** 26 map, Sources—map temperatures from NASA Goddard Institute for Space Studies (NASA/GISS); **NationalGeographicStock.com:** James Balog: 36; John Burcham: 43; Peter Essick: 12, 18-19, 20-21, 22, 25, 34; Melissa Farlow: 11; Natalie B. Fobes: 39 bottom; Bill Hatcher: 45 top; Ralph Lee Hopkins: 16 top; Mattias Klum: 14; David Liittschwager: 35 all; Sarah Leen: 54; O. Louis Mazzatenta: 6; David McLain: 7-8; NASA: 10 all; Richard Nowitz: 45 center; Paul Nicklen: 5; Kip Ross: 28 top; Cyril Ruoso/Minden Pictures: 45 bottom; Maria Stenzel, 14 inset; Mark Thiessen: 37, 49 bottom; **Pelamis Wave Power Ltd:** 44; **Roy Gumpel/Touch Productions Ltd:** 16 right, 28 right, 38 right, 48 right, 58 right; **Shutterstock:** Lee O'Dell: 33; Specta: 34 inset; **Sipa Press:** Arne Nevra/ SCANPIX/: Cover; **Solar Decathlon:** Kaye Evans-Lutterodt: 47; **Tim Helweg-Larsen:** 29 bottom.

PUBLISHED BY THE
NATIONAL GEOGRAPHIC SOCIETY

John M. Fahey, Jr.,
President and Chief Executive Officer

Gilbert M. Grosvenor, *Chairman of the Board*

Tim T. Kelly, *President, Global Media Group*

John Q. Griffin, *President, Publishing*

Nina D. Hoffman, *Executive Vice President;
President, Book Publishing Group*

PREPARED BY THE BOOK DIVISION

Nancy Laties Feresten,
Vice President, Editor in Chief, Children's Books

Bea Jackson, *Director of Design and Illustrations,
Children's Books*

Amy Shields, *Executive Editor, Series, Children's Books*

Jennifer Emmett, *Executive Editor, Reference and Solo,
Children's Books*

Carl Mehler, *Director of Maps*

STAFF FOR THIS BOOK

Jennifer Emmett, *Editor*

Lori Epstein, *Illustrations Editor*

Bea Jackson, *Art Director and Designer*

David M. Seager and Jim Hiscott, *Designers*

Jennifer Eaton, *Editorial Intern*

Lewis Bassford, *Production Project Manager*

Jennifer A. Thornton, *Managing Editor*

Grace Hill, *Associate Managing Editor*

R. Gary Colbert, *Production Director*

Susan Borke, *Legal and Business Affairs*

MANUFACTURING
AND QUALITY MANAGEMENT

Christopher A. Liedel, *Chief Financial Officer*

Phillip L. Schlosser, *Vice President*

Chris Brown, *Technical Director*

Monika Lynde, *Manager*

Founded in 1888, the National Geographic Society is one of the largest nonprofit scientific and educational organizations in the world. It reaches more than 285 million people worldwide each month through its official journal, NATIONAL GEOGRAPHIC, and its four other magazines; the National Geographic Channel; television documentaries; radio programs; films; books; videos and DVDs; maps; and interactive media. National Geographic has funded more than 8,000 scientific research projects and supports an education program combating geographic illiteracy.

For more information, please call 1-800-NGS LINE (647-5463) or write to the following address:

NATIONAL GEOGRAPHIC SOCIETY
1145 17th Street N.W., Washington, D.C. 20036-4688 U.S.A.

Visit us online at www.nationalgeographic.com/books

For librarians and teachers: www.ngchildrensbooks.org

More for kids from National Geographic: kids.nationalgeographic.com

For information about special discounts for bulk purchases, please contact National Geographic Books
Special Sales: ngspecsales@ngs.org

For rights or permissions inquiries, please contact National Geographic Books Subsidiary Rights:
ngbookrights@ngs.org